NOW THAT YOU CAN WALK, GO GET ME A BEER

A BOOK FOR DADS

THE CARTOON BANK, INC.

A FIRESIDE BOOK
PUBLISHED BY SIMON & SCHUSTER

NEW YORK   LONDON   TORONTO   SYDNEY   TOKYO   SINGAPORE

FIRESIDE
ROCKEFELLER CENTER
1230 AVENUE OF THE AMERICAS
NEW YORK, NEW YORK 10020

FIRESIDE AND COLOPHON ARE REGISTERED
TRADEMARKS OF SIMON & SCHUSTER INC.

MANUFACTURED IN THE UNITED STATES OF AMERICA

10 9 8 7 6 5 4 3 2 1

LIBRARY OF CONGRESS CATALOGING-IN-PUBLICATION DATA
IS AVAILABLE

ISBN: 0-671-87962-6

THIS BOOK IS SET IN THE COMIC BOOK FONT, COPYRIGHT© 1994
VANGUARD MEDIA, INC., (212) 242-5317.

THE CARTOONISTS

GEORGE ABBOTT

DONNA BARSTOW

ROZ CHAST

FRANK COTHAM

MICHAEL CRAWFORD

LEO CULLUM

JOE DATOR

BORIS DRUCKER

ED FRASCINO

MORT GERBERG

ANNE GIBBONS

LIZ HABERFELD

WILLIAM HAEFELI

MARIAN HENLEY

JOHN JONIK

BRUCE ERIC KAPLAN

ARNIE LEVIN

ROBERT MANKOFF

PETER S. MUELLER

JOHN O'BRIEN

LIBBY REID

BERNARD SCHOENBAUM

DAVID SIPRESS

MICK STEVENS

PETER VEY

JACK ZIEGLER

ABOUT THE "AUTHOR"

THE CARTOON BANK IS A COMPUTERIZED
CARTOON STOCK HOUSE FEATURING MORE
THAN 10,000 CARTOONS BY THE COUNTRY'S
TOP CARTOONISTS. ORIGINAL ARTWORK,
FIRST-TIME PRINTING RIGHTS, REPRINT
RIGHTS, LICENSING RIGHTS, CUSTOM
CARTOONS, AND LOANS OF ORIGINALS FOR
EXHIBITION ARE ALL AVAILABLE FOR
PURCHASE. TO ORDER ANY OF THE
CARTOONS IN THIS COLLECTION, OR TO
RECEIVE A FREE SELECTION OF CARTOONS
ON ANY TOPIC BY FAX, CALL
1-800-897-TOON.

A MESSAGE FROM THE PRESIDENT
(OF THE CARTOON BANK, INC.)

MY FELLOW AMERICANS, IN THESE TIMES, WHEN THERE IS SO MUCH HANDWRINGING ABOUT DYSFUNCTIONAL FAMILIES, WE AT THE CARTOON BANK ARE PROUD TO PRESENT A BOOK THAT CELEBRATES FAMILIES AND THEIR DYSFUNCTIONAL FAMILY VALUES.

HERE ARE 120 HILARIOUS, UPROARIOUS, THESAURIOUS CARTOONS WITH A SIMPLE MESSAGE TO ALL PARENTS AND KIDS: "DON'T WORRY, BE FUNNY." FOLLOW THIS SIMPLE, EVEN SIMPLE-MINDED CREDO AND I GUARANTEE YOU WILL BE 100 PERCENT SATISFIED. IF NOT, TRY 75 PERCENT—THAT OFTEN WORKS.

EACH OF THESE AWARD-WINNING CARTOONS (THE ONE ON PAGE 32, FOR EXAMPLE, WON THE CROIX DE GUERRE) HAS BEEN PERSONALLY INSPECTED BY AN OFFICIAL OF THE CARTOON BANK, AND HAS BEEN FOUND TO SUPPLY THE RECOMMENDED DAILY ALLOWANCE OF HUMOR AS WELL AS TRACE AMOUNTS OF DANGEROUS MINERALS.

FURTHERMORE, AS PRESIDENT OF THE CARTOON BANK, I CAN PERSONALLY ATTEST THAT THESE CARTOONS ARE FUN FOR THE WHOLE FAMILY, PESKY NEIGHBORS, AND EVEN TOTAL STRANGERS WHO FIND THIS BOOK WHILE RANSACKING YOUR PERSONAL BELONGINGS.

I CAN ALSO ATTEST THAT THE SUBJECT MATTER OF THIS BOOK IS A NATURAL ONE FOR CARTOONISTS, BECAUSE WE ARE CHILDREN AT HEART AND HAVE TO PARENT OURSELVES EVERY DAY. EACH OF US HAS NEVER LET THAT LITTLE CHILD WITHIN US DIE. THIS, OF COURSE, IS SELFISH ON OUR PART BECAUSE IF THE LITTLE CHILD WITHIN US DIES, IT STARTS TO ROT AND THEN REALLY STINK.

A FINAL WORD: AS GREAT AS THIS BOOK IS, IT SHOULD NOT BE USED AS A SUBSTITUTE FOR MORE TRADITIONAL CHILD-REARING TEXTS OR AS A REPLACEMENT FOR A PROGRAM OF CONSCIENTIOUS ORAL HYGIENE.

ANOTHER FINAL WORD: PERMISSION TO REPRINT ANY OF THESE CARTOONS MAY BE OBTAINED BY CALLING THE CARTOON BANK IN PRESTIGIOUS HASTINGS, NEW YORK, WHERE ALL THESE IMAGES ARE STORED ON AN ELECTRONIC DEVICE NO LARGER THAN THE SOFT SPOT ON A BABY'S HEAD.

THANK YOU, AND GOD BLESS YOU.

BOB MANKOFF
PRESIDENT
OF THE CARTOON BANK, INC.

Oooglie oooglie googlie googlie...
Who is this person? Where's the one with the milk??
SIPRESS

"ONE OF THEM IS, I BELIEVE, MINE."

"DID YOU RECOGNIZE THAT, POP? IT WAS THE 'MINUTE WALTZ.' I'VE GOT IT DOWN TO 23 SECONDS FLAT."

"SEE? I TOLD YOU IT WAS ONLY A MATTER OF TIME BEFORE BARNEY AND ALL OF HIS ILK WENT BAD."

"DON'T GET ME WRONG. YOU'VE BEEN GREAT THESE LAST EIGHT MONTHS. BUT DON'T YOU THINK YOU SHOULD BE PAYING MORE ATTENTION TO YOUR OWN WIFE AND CHILD."

"I'LL TRADE YOU TED WILLIAMS AND NOLAN RYAN FOR THE POLAROIDS YOUR DAD TOOK OF YOUR MOM."

"AND SO THE BIG BAD WOLF ATE LITTLE RED RIDING HOOD, HANSEL AND GRETEL, CINDERELLA, AND THE THREE LITTLE PIGS, AND THAT WAS THE END OF FAIRY TALES FOREVER. NOW GOOD NIGHT!"

"MY FATHER WAKES UP THE SUN EVERY MORNING. WHAT DOES YOUR FATHER DO?"

"RACHEL! IF YOU CAN'T EVEN STAY FOCUSED ON SPREADING PEAT MOSS, HOW DO YOU EXPECT TO GET INTO LAW SCHOOL?"

"IF THIS WERE A SITCOM, YOUR ANTICS WOULD BE DELIGHTFULLY AMUSING. UNFORTUNATELY FOR YOU, THIS IS NOT A SITCOM."

"... AND TO MY CHILDREN, LUCILLE AND EDWARD, I BEQUEATH ALL MY INSECURITIES AND NEUROSES...."

"CONGRATULATIONS, MR. PACKARD, I'VE DELIVERED YOU A FINE BABY BOY. WOULD YOU SIGN FOR IT, PLEASE?"

"YOUR MOTHER WANTS TO GO SOUTH WHEN WE RETIRE, WHICH SUITS ME NO END, BECAUSE I WANT TO STAY HERE."

"HUSH NOW, CHILDREN. DADDY IS HAVING HIS LITTLE QUIET TIME."

"DAD, WAIT! YOU'RE LEAVING THE HOUSE DRESSED LIKE THAT? AND YOUR LAST NAME IS THE SAME AS MINE?"

"REALLY HOWARD! YOU'RE JUST LIKE YOUR FATHER."

"IF YOUR MOTHER HAS NOTHING FURTHER TO ADD, WE MAY NOW CONSIDER THIS STAFF MEETING CLOSED."

"THEY'RE HATCHING! QUICK, ALBERT, GET THE CAMCORDER!"

D. Barstow

"HEY, WOULD YOU KIDS MIND HOLDING DOWN THE
QUALITY-TIME RACKET?"

"I HOPE YOU DON'T EXPECT MUCH SYMPATHY FROM YOUR
GRANDPARENTS. WHO DO YOU THINK RAISED US
TO BE LIKE THIS?"

"WELL, WE DIDN'T CATCH ANY FLY BALLS, BUT JOEY CAUGHT HIS FIRST METEORITE."

"I GOTTA GO PLAY WITH MY DOLL NOW, SO THAT I'LL BE A REALLY GREAT DAD SOMEDAY."

"SON, I'VE GIVEN THIS A LOT OF THOUGHT. THESE ARE YOUR
FORMATIVE YEARS, SO STAY AWAY FROM ME
AS MUCH AS POSSIBLE."

"FIRST THE STORK, NOW THE BIRDS AND THE BEES—WHEN DO WE GET DOWN TO THE NITTY-GRITTY, DAD?"

FAMILY OUTING

"GOING SHOPPING WITH YOUR MOTHER? I'LL STAY HERE AND CARRY ON A PLEASANT SILENCE WITH YOUR FATHER."

"SUCK DOWN THOSE VEGETABLES, SON, LEST YOU GROW UP
TO BE A POLITICALLY INCORRECT MEAT-AND-POTATOES MAN
LIKE YOUR DAD USED TO BE."

"WE KNOW YOU'VE GOT THE RAW TALENT, CORLISS, BUT DO YOU HAVE THE REQUISITE DESIRE? WELL, DO YOU?"

"THE CONDOM BROKE. HOW ABOUT YOU?"

"I ALREADY HAVE LOTS OF DADS. CAN'T WE JUST BE FRIENDS?"

"RAGE MAY BE THE BUZZWORD FOR THE NINETIES, DICKIE, BUT PLEASE, NOT AT THE DINNER TABLE."

"SON, I THINK YOU'RE OLD ENOUGH NOW TO KNOW ABOUT THE BIRDS AND THE BIRDS."

"YOU'RE NOT FOLLOWING IN MY FOOTSTEPS, LEONARD."

"YOU'RE A GOOD BOY, SON, BUT YOUR MOTHER AND I HAVE TALKED IT OVER AND WE THINK THAT A RAISE IN YOUR ALLOWANCE TO FOUR FIGURES IS EXCESSIVE."

"THIS ABOVE ALL, JONATHAN, TO THY OWN SELF AND LEADING ECONOMIC INDICATORS BE TRUE."

"WE DIDN'T WANT TO SURPRISE YOU TOO MUCH, DAD."

"BECAUSE I'M A SOVEREIGN, AND A SOVEREIGN IS ALLOWED
NOT TO EAT HIS SPINACH IF HE DOESN'T WANT TO."

"I CAN'T HELP YOU WITH YOUR HOMEWORK RIGHT NOW, SON.
DADDY'S GOT WORK TO DO."

"I'M AFRAID WE'VE CONFIRMED THAT INTELLIGENCE OFTEN SKIPS A GENERATION."

"SEE, SON? HE'S NOT GONE. HE JUST TURNED INTO 'SPLASHY THE PUDDLEMAN.'"

"CONGRATULATIONS! I'VE NEVER HEARD A FALSEHOOD
SO WELL TOLD."

"WE'VE VOTED TO SEND OUT FOR FOOD."

"GREETINGS, STOCKHOLDERS."

"NOT BAD, DAD, BUT HOW ABOUT TEACHING ME THE VALUE OF A TWENTY INSTEAD?"

"SORRY, BUT I CAN'T BE LATE FOR DINNER AGAIN. MY POP'S BEEN THREATENING ECONOMIC SANCTIONS."

"REMEMBER, JASON, IT'S NEVER TOO EARLY TO BEGIN CULTIVATING FRIENDS WHO MAY SOMEDAY DO YOU SOME GOOD."

"IF YOU ASK ME, THIS KID ISN'T LOST. HIS PARENTS JUST MADE A RUN FOR IT."

"I DID GO TO SLEEP, BUT IT DIDN'T TAKE."

"WELL, MAYBE IF YOU SPENT A LITTLE MORE TIME WITH YOUR FAMILY, YOU'D SEE SOMEONE YOU RECOGNIZED!"

"I HOPE YOU'RE HAPPY, HAROLD. YOUR MIDNIGHT SNACK
WAS SAMMY'S SCIENCE PROJECT."

"HE'S MAKING A LIST AND CHECKING IT TWICE. ALTHOUGH HE DOESN'T NEED TO, WHAT WITH HIS NEW SOFTWARE."

"DO YOU REMEMBER ANY OF THOSE THINGS PEOPLE SAID
WE'D TELL OUR GRANDKIDS SOMEDAY?"

"YOU HAVE THE RIGHT TO REMAIN SILENT . . ."

WHAT MUST THEY DO TO THAT CHILD?

"YOU SAY YOU'RE THE BOSS HERE, BUT THAT'S WHAT MOM SAYS SHE IS. I'D LIKE TO SEE AN ORGANIZATIONAL CHART."

"DAD, I THINK I'M READY FOR OUR LITTLE TALK ABOUT THE BULLS AND THE BEARS."

"THE WEASEL REPRESENTS THE FORCES OF EVIL AND THE DUCK THE FORCES OF GOOD, A SURROGATE FOR AMERICAN AIR AND NAVAL SUPERIORITY."

"HAVE A STICK OF GUM. I JUST BECAME A FATHER."

"I DID ASK HER AND SHE SAID TO ASK YOU WHERE
I CAME FROM."

"I'M DOING GREAT. BY NEXT WEEK YOU CAN START TELLING ME HOW THINGS ARE AT HOME."

"SORRY TO GET YOU OUT OF SCHOOL EARLY, SON, BUT I
NEED YOUR HELP WITH THIS COMPUTER."

"HOW DO YOU FEEL ABOUT THIS NEW TREND
OF PARENTING?"

"WITH ALL THIS RAIN WE'VE BEEN HAVING LATELY, THE KIDS ARE REALLY SPROUTING OUT THERE."

"SOMEDAY, SON, ALL THIS AND MORE WILL BE YOURS,
IF YOU REMEMBER TO ALWAYS SUPPORT THE
REPUBLICAN PARTY."

"YOU CAN DO BETTER."

"YOU SHOULD DECIDE FOR YOURSELF WHAT'S IMPORTANT
IN LIFE AND THEN FIGURE OUT A WAY TO PAY FOR IT."

"WHEN WE WERE YOUNG WE DIDN'T HAVE THOSE FANCY TOYS. WE HAD TO DEVELOP OUR IMAGINATIONS."

"WE'RE VERY PROUD OF SEAN. HE'S ONLY IN THE SIXTH GRADE, BUT HE'S MAKING WISE-GUY REMARKS AT A COLLEGE LEVEL."

"DON'T TELL ME IT'S GOING TO BE *TREASURE ISLAND AGAIN.*"

"I'M HAVING LUNCH WITH MY INNER CHILD."

"SOMETIMES, I THINK EDWARD'S CARRYING HIS ROLE MODEL
A BIT TOO FAR."

"FOR PETE'S SAKE, DAD, IT'S JUST ANOTHER BABY TOOTH.
IT'S NOTHING TO GET ALL WEEPY ABOUT."

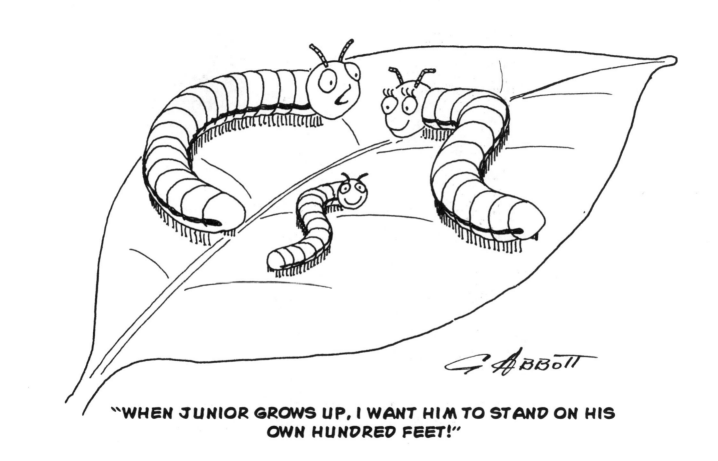

"WHEN JUNIOR GROWS UP, I WANT HIM TO STAND ON HIS OWN HUNDRED FEET!"

"YOU ARE OLD ENOUGH TO CHOOSE, CHRISTOPHER. DO YOU WANT TO LIVE WITH *MOMMY* OR *DADDY?*"

Doesn't it BOTHER you that we're leaving the baby while we go off for the weekend?
Not really.
You're not WORRIED?
No, I'm sure he'll be fine!
How can we REALLY share the responsibilities of parenthood...
..if you don't share the GUILT?!!
©Anne Gibbons

"TELL ME AGAIN, FATHER. WHAT ARE MY OPTIONS IN RELATION TO THIS BROCCOLI?"

"WHOA, DAD! HOW ABOUT IF I EXERCISE MY POWER OF ATTORNEY HERE?"

"JUST THINK OF IT AS A BRIEF INTERLUDE IN, AS OPPOSED TO A MAJOR DISRUPTION OF, YOUR LIFE."

"EXCUSE ME FOR SOUNDING LIKE A JEWISH MOTHER, BUT
MAY I POINT OUT THAT YOUR KID IS GETTING WET."

"I BET MY DAD'S CHOLESTEROL LEVEL IS HIGHER
THAN YOUR DAD'S."

"DON'T COMPLAIN AND DON'T EXPLAIN AND SOMEDAY, SON, YOU COULD BE PRESIDENT."

"... AND SO THE PRINCESS AND THE PRINCE LIVED HAPPILY EVER AFTER. THE END. NOW GET SOME SLEEP. WE WANT YOU TO BE FRESH AS A DAISY FOR YOUR FIRST DAY OF COLLEGE TOMORROW."

"GEE, DAD, INSTEAD OF DRUMMING AND CHANTING TOGETHER, CAN'T WE JUST WATCH THE SERIES?"

1
HOW CAN YOU DO THIS TO US??!!
2
Who said that?? Is my father here?
SIPRESS

"DON'T LET ME BOTHER YOU. I'M CAPTAIN AVENGER TODAY, WHICH MEANS I'M INVISIBLE."

"IS IT OK TO DISCRIMINATE AGAINST BIGOTS?"

"I KEPT A SMALL PERCENTAGE OF YOUR ALLOWANCE FOR ADMINISTRATIVE COSTS."

"DEAR SANTA: DON'T YOU JUST HATE IT WHEN PEOPLE USE WORDS LIKE *GOOD* OR *BAD?*"

"I WISH YOU'D TRY HARDER TO LIKE SCHOOL, JEREMY. IT'S COSTING DADDY A BUNDLE."

"IF YOU REALLY WANT THE PUPPY, TELL MOM YOU'RE SAVING FOR AN IGUANA OR SOMETHING..."

"YOU'RE NOT REAL EXPERIENCED AT THIS FATHER
BUSINESS, ARE YOU?"

"SEE WHAT DADDY HAS FOR YOU, IF YOU STOP CRYING?"